GW00458587

# Let's
# Collect
# Cottagewares

⌐ ● ⌐

# Let's
# Collect
# Cottagewares

Virginia Brisco

Published by Virginia and Bill Brisco
Inglefield, 218 Sandridge Road, St. Albans, Herts. AL1 4AL.

First published 1992
by Virginia and Bill Brisco


Text and photographs: Virginia Brisco

Design and Layout: Keith Poole

## COVER PHOTOGRAPHS

Front Cover: Watcombe oval tray 14″ (36cms) wide. c. 1930

Inside Front Cover: Watcombe faience vase 14″ (36cms) tall
decorated with a view of Crazy Kate's Cottage, Clovelly. c. 1909.

Inside Back Cover: Watcombe 6½″ (16.5cms) tall jug finely
decorated in slips with a street scene, c. 1935. The motto on the
reverse is "Work On Hope On, Self help is noble schooling, You
do your best and leave the rest, to God Almighty's ruling."

© 1992 Virginia and Bill Brisco

ISBN  0  95200045  0  X

Typeset, printed and bound in Great Britain by
Redwood Press Limited, Melksham, Wiltshire

# Preface

This book evolved from a short talk I gave on "How to identify Torquay Cottagewares" at the Torquay Pottery Collectors Society Symposium in October 1991. Since the publication of "Torquay Mottowares" in 1989 many people have become enthusiastic collectors of mottowares, in particular of the most popular decoration, the Devon cottage. Clearly these collectors want more information on how to identify cottagewares and the range of items made, and this book aims to fulfil that need. In addition to cottage mottowares, there are sections on pigment decorated "faience" wares and moulded cottagewares which became so popular in the 1930's, plus a short outline of some twenty Devon and Dorset potteries that made these wares.

# Acknowledgements

This book would not have been possible without the help of many people. For the loan of pots for the photographs I should like to thank Mrs Stacy Asher, Mr and Mrs Derek Barber, Mrs Joan Leatherland, Mr Sydney Reed, Mrs Joyce Stonelake, Mr and Mrs Ron Wood.

Many old potters, or those with Torquay pottery connections, have given freely of their time to talk to me and bring the potteries to life; I should particularly like to thank Mrs Winifred Anniss, the late Mr Roy Blackler, Miss Joan Collard, Mrs Joyce Harfield, Mr Cyril Lemon, Mr Leslie Manley, the late Mrs Elsie Medland, Mr and Mrs Arthur Miller, Mr John Tilstone, Mrs Edna White, Mr Cyril Wilson. I am also grateful to Mr John Tilstone and Miss Margaret Broderick for making copies of Watcombe Pottery catalogues available to me, and to Mr Gary Rook for help with the identification of some Crown Dorset cottagewares.

Finally, my thanks go to Keith Poole for the Design and Layout of the book as well as helpful advice, and to my husband Bill for encouragement, patience, advice, and for typing the manuscript. Also to the many members of the Torquay Pottery Collectors Society who have shared their pots with me over the last fifteen years.

# Introduction

IT is often said that an Englishman's home is his castle yet today most "Englishmen" dream, not of castles, but of living in a cottage in the country. Country cottages evoke images of peace and tranquillity and, for people unable to live in such places, some of these feelings can be satisfied by acquiring pictures of rural landscapes be it an oil painting or the more humble cottages scratched on mottowares.

The image of the countryside as a haven of peace and tranquillity has only developed over the past 150 years or so. Before that, when Britain was still an agricultural country, rural life meant dirt (either dust in summer or mud in winter) and danger from the perils of highwaymen or robbers. For isolated farming communities, the only relief from work came with church festivals such as Christmas, Easter, or the Harvest Supper. To provincial people, especially the rapidly growing middle classes, towns were perceived as desirable places to live because they were full of "life" – witness the growth of cities such as Bath; or Regent's Park in London. Towns had so much appeal because one could meet people there, enjoy cultural pursuits such as music or plays, and buy the consumer goods which were widely available thanks to industrialisation and improved communications.

However, as the Industrial Revolution gained pace more and more rural workers flocked to the towns to seek higher wages in factories. Rows and rows of terraced "back to back" houses were built to accommodate them but the lack of sanitation and overcrowding soon led to dirt and disease. Towns grew into big cities which were polluted from smokey factory chimneys and the constant noise of machinery.

By the middle of Queen Victoria's reign the majority of people lived in towns and generations of children had grown up without seeing woods, fields or farm animals in their everyday lives. These were the people who began to dream about escaping from the noise and dirt of town life and getting back to nature in the countryside. In art and literature this new mood was reflected in the rise of the Romantic Movement, a reaction against industrialisation which looked nostalgically back to a Golden Age of Agriculture when traditional values prevailed. In painting, this Movement was epitomised by the growth of rural scenes depicting pretty country cottages with roses round the door, and wistful peasants – they may be wearing ragged clothes but they are always clean and well fed! By the end of Victoria's reign such sentimentality had mass appeal and picturesque scenes adorned the walls of many working class homes.

The Romantic Movement encouraged interest in the crafts of the Middle Ages, especially through the efforts of people such as William Morris and the Art Workers Guild. The Arts and Crafts Movement encouraged the development of traditional crafts and skills which, it was feared, were being lost due to mass production. This provided the impetus for a whole new industry of potting centred around Torquay in South Devon.

Before the Industrial Revolution country potters supplied the needs of their local communities but most of these had died out with the advent of cheap mass produced wares. However, in 1869 a new band of fine red clay was discovered in the grounds of Watcombe House, near Torquay, and its owner, Dr. G. J. Allen decided to erect a pottery to provide employment for local people. Within a few years the popularity of these hand crafted wares had increased and other small potteries were established in the area to meet the demand – their products became known generically as Devonshire ware or Torquay Pottery.

During the latter nineteenth century Torquay and its environs became a popular winter retreat for the middle classes on account of its mild climate. These were the very people who expounded the cause of "arts and crafts" and had the money to indulge their "good taste", often by purchasing the products of the local potteries, which they had perhaps witnessed being made. The potteries were keen to capitalise on this tourist trade, and what more natural than that they should enhance their wares by decorating them with local views, especially the rural scenes which visitors found so appealing.

Fig. 2 Cottage decorations by the Torquay Pottery. Tall vase c. 1910, small model of a cottage c. 1915, vase with moulded flower handles and coal scuttle c. 1930.

Fig. 1 Watcombe faience style decoration. Biscuit barrel c. 1907; cup and saucer c. 1910; dressing table tray c. 1907; vase c. 1930; Moorland cottage vase c. 1926.

# Faience Wares

THE earliest rural scenes made in the Torquay potteries date from c.1905 – they are finely decorated in natural coloured pigments on a cream background under a clear glaze. This type of decoration was known as "faience". An advertisement placed in the Pottery Gazette of September 1905 by the Watcombe Pottery described their "newest" decoration which was between deep green borders: "A light grounded band runs round the pieces, while farm buildings, animals and figures and scenes are portrayed on the band". By 1907 these were described as "Devonshire scenes" and prominent amongst the vases shown in the March issue of the Pottery Gazette were the prototypes of the later cottagewares – these depict a typical Devon cottage viewed from the corner with a sloping path going up to the door, the cottage being surrounded by trees. (see fig. 4).

In addition to the Watcombe Pottery, Longpark and the Torquay Pottery also made faience cottagewares during the Edwardian period; so too did the Crown Dorset Pottery at Poole; this pottery was established in 1905 by Charles Collard who had previously worked in the Torquay potteries and many of their early wares were decorated in the same style. Indeed, unmarked examples can easily be confused with Torquay pottery by the inexperienced collector.

Early faience wares show a great diversity in style of decoration. Almost every conceivable style of Devon cottage is shown, reflecting the individuality of the decorators. Cottages are

Fig. 3 Crown Dorset "udder" vase decorated in faience style c.1907. Note how the three spouts are in a row, which was typical of the Dorset Pottery; Devon pottery udder vases had four or five spouts.

Fig. 4 Selection of faience wares from the Watcombe Pottery. The biscuit barrel has a silver plated rim, cover and twisted handle; it depicts the type of cottage illustrated in the Pottery Gazette in March 1907, the others are slightly later c.1910.

shown in isolation, or in groups, and some are surrounded by a colourful profusion of garden flowers. Other cottages are depicted against a village background with a church tower, or nestling beside a lake, or a river with a watermill. The most common colour for the borders was dark green, either painted or sprayed, but Longpark often used beige borders and the Torquay Pottery sometimes favoured tan (see fig. 2).

Cottage scenes were applied to a wide variety of items. A Watcombe catalogue c.1910 illustrates nine different shapes of vases all of which were made in six different sizes ranging from $4^{1}/_{2}''$ to 14″ tall. Other items in the catalogue were jardinieres, tobacco jars, cream bowls, jugs and three different shapes of teapots. Also made were dressing table trays, hat pin holders, cups and saucers, biscuit barrels and pen trays.

Many faience decorated items were made as special orders and some of these were silver plated. An example is the biscuit barrel shown in fig. 4 which has a silver plated rim and cover and a delicately twisted handle. Condiments sets had plated stoppers and lids, while egg cups were sold in sets of four in metal stands. Some items were very large such as a magnificent plant pot and pedestal set three feet tall; the pot was decorated with two Devonshire cottages whilst the stand was adorned with cows. Many pot and pedestal sets were made as gifts for employees of the potteries when they got married and were decorated according to the wishes of the bride and groom.

Fig. 5 Selection of pigment painted wares. Left to right: squat jug moulded in relief to show the First and Last House at Land's End, painted in pigment over the moulding, by Torquay Pottery; mug made by Bovey Pottery Co.; vase with view of cottages at Cockington by Longpark; pen tray by Longpark; Crown Dorset jug; Torquay Pottery jug depicting cottage with timber on end wall.

By the time of World War I cottage-wares had mass appeal but as great quantities of pots were made so the quality of decoration began to decline, a process which escalated during the war when many potters were called up for military service. Faience cottagewares became more stylised with a single cottage set amongst trees being the norm. It was also about this time that the potteries began to experiment with a much cheaper version of cottagewares where the cottage was drawn in sgraffito and slip with a motto scratched on the reverse. Mottowa es were 30% to 50% cheaper than faience wares and the originality of the mottoes compensated for the lack of originality in the crudely executed cottage. These cottagewares soon became the "bread and butter lines" of the potteries, although some faience wares were made up until the 1930's.

During the interwar years the influence of the Art Deco Movement brought a fashion for more colourful art pottery. Pre-war country view ware with its borders of dark green, beige or tan was too sombre for the jazz age so these were livened up by the use of much brighter colours. In March 1926 Watcombe placed an advertisement in the Pottery Gazette to publicise their "new Moor-

Fig. 6 Watcombe faience water jug with a cottage beside a bridge c. 1908.

Fig. 7 Barton plate decorated with a moonlight scene on a blue ground under a clear glaze. c. 1930.

Fig. 8 Cottages on coloured backgrounds; Left, Watcombe teapot with winter cottage on a blue ground c. 1958; Torquay Pottery moonlight scene under a pink glaze c. 1920; Barton moonlight scene on blue ground c. 1930.

land Cottage" which depicted a typical Devon Cottage surrounded by a bright mauve sprayed border, presumably representing moorland heather (see fig. 1). Another version showed the cottage on a cream ground set between very thin bands of mauve pigment. Sometimes bright yellow or pink sprayed borders were used instead.

The Torquay Pottery brought out a range of vases painted in brighter colours which had handles moulded in the form of multi-coloured flower heads (fig. 2). Another line depicted a black painted scene of cottages and trees under a deep pink glaze which produced a very dramatic effect. The Barton Pottery, one of several new potteries established after the Great War, specialised in moonlit scenes done on a Royal blue background under a clear glaze; these are highly sought by collectors because of their superb quality glazing. Watcombe used a warm amber glaze to give the effect of cottages set against the glow of the evening sun; this technique was used on pigment and slip decorated cottages although in some cases the amber glaze has turned the green trees into a muddy black colour which is rather sombre.

Fig. 9 Three items made by the Bovey Pottery Company in the 1930s. White clay painted in pigments.

Fig. 10 Crown Dorset faience jug.

A few faience wares were still being made in the mid 1930's but these were poorly executed compared to their earlier counterparts. The Watcombe Pottery made ashtrays and cream bowls with pigment painted cottages but these were done in the same style as the mottowares and even carried a motto painted in black. Normally, faience wares did not have mottoes, except perhaps a place name. The Bovey Pottery Company brought out a new range of cottagewares in the 1930's; these are made of white clay and depict a crudely painted cottage situated between trees. Often these are stamped "Dartmoor Ware" on the base.

# Mottowares

MOTTOWARES are the most common form of cottage decoration and were so popular that to many collectors cottagewares are synonymous with Torquay Pottery. These can easily be distinguished from faience wares because they are painted in slips as opposed to pigments. Slip is a creamy mixture of clay and water to which colour has been added; it is painted on with a brush or trailed on from a piping bag or similar tool, very much as one would ice a cake. Slips enable the decoration to be done much more quickly although the finished result is cruder than the finely decorated faience wares. Sometimes all the decoration and motto was painted in slips, but more commonly it was a combination of slips and sgraffito. The pots were usually made of red clay then dipped in cream slip to form a uniform background colour. The outline of the cottage was scratched through the slip using a 6″ nail to expose the red clay, this process being known as sgraffito. Slips were applied to embellish the cottage and to form the decorative border. Sgraffito mottoes were applied, and often place names too; in the late 1950's and early 1960's place names were

sometimes transfer printed. Occasionally white clay was used to make the pots in which case the mottoes were painted in brown slips or pigment, or transfer printed as on some late Dartmouth wares.

Cottagewares evolved from two sources; the popularity of mottowares and the growing interest in rural scenes as a form of decoration. Mottowares had been made in South Devon since the 1880's at the Aller Vale Pottery when mottoes were applied to pots decorated with stylised flowers or scrolls. By the turn of the century Watcombe, Hart & Moist and Longpark were also making mottowares, the most popular decorations being ships, cockerels and a scroll decoration similar to Prince of Wales feathers which became known as the Scandy (or Scando) pattern. These wares had wide appeal and the Pottery Gazette of August 1910 noted that "Devonshire mottoed ware enjoys a popularity far beyond the limit of the county", much of the appeal being its "quaint inscriptions" and "old time phrases". The potteries vied with each other to produce more and more useful and ornamental articles or novelties

Fig. 11 Selection of late cottagewares. Left to right: Babbacombe jug; Watcombe ashtray depicting Old Mother Hubbard's Cottage done in bright contemporary colours; Dartmouth plate decorated with cottage having blue dot windows; St. Marychurch vinegar bottle; Dartmouth cheese or muffin dish. Plate 10″ (25cms) diameter.

Fig. 12 Selection of typical mottowares. Water jug and hat pin holder by Watcombe; coffee pot, candlestick and shaving mug by Longpark.

to satisfy the ever expanding market.

The earliest slip decorated cottages appear to have originated at the Hart & Moist Pottery at Exeter in 1912. An advertisement placed in the Pottery Gazette of January 1913 illustrated a teapot, sugar bowl and milk jug decorated with a cottage set amongst trees; the cottage had a timbered end wall which became the typical "house-style" at Hart & Moist. Although cottages later became very popular, Hart & Moist examples are quite hard to find; of those that have been seen, all were entirely slip decorated, the only sgraffito being used for the lettering. Soon afterwards other potteries followed suit and produced their own version of cottagewares. The Watcombe Pottery, which probably produced more cottagewares than all the other potteries put together, are believed to have introduced the design about 1915.

Cottagewares were produced for over fifty years from c.1912 to the early 1960's, and at least fifteen potteries in the South Devon/Dorset area made them. Collectors should also note that other potteries made similar wares too,

e.g. Powell, Buckley in North Wales; whilst these are quite attractive, they are not Torquay Pottery. In the past few years some individual potters, mostly ex Watcombe employees, have started making cottagewares again to satisfy a growing interest in collecting. These wares are backstamped with the potters mark but some dealers have been known to claim they are "old Torquay pottery". They are not "old" of course, although they are Torquay Pottery.

The range of cottagewares made was enormous, both in terms of style of cottage, and the items made. Each of the potteries developed their own "house style" although within each style there were many variations, and some decorators had their own individual styles. Harry Crute, for instance, favoured inglenook chimneys and he produced these both at Watcombe and Dartmouth potteries. The potteries had a policy of marking their wares with their factory of origin but many pots escaped this process, or the marks are so feint they are unreadable. A selection of marks is shown in this book although collectors are advised to consult the Torquay Pottery Mark Book, published by the T.P.C.S. for a comprehensive guide to marks.

Fig. 13 Hart & Moist milk jug and sugar bowl. The shapes are typical of this pottery but the style of cottage is most unusual and very few examples have been seen.

# Identifying Unmarked Cottagewares

COLLECTORS like to know the origin of their unmarked pots and with experience most items can be attributed fairly accurately. Identifying features include the style of cottage, type of tool used for sgraffito work and style of lettering used for mottoes. Sometimes the consistency of the clay can give clues to pottery of origin, for instance, Longpark clay is often very dark and Hart & Moist clay is speckled and

Fig. 14 Typical Crown Dorset lettering. Reverse of Fig. 3.

"gritty". Many shapes were common to all the potteries (the 1476 shaped teapot being a prime example) but some were peculiar to one, or maybe two potteries; collectors can only learn individual shapes by studying lots of pots or researching old catalogues and advertisements.

The drawings and photographs illustrate typical features of particular potteries and should be used as an overall guide to identification. Some potteries produced so little cottagewares that a "house style" did not evolve. There are also many "exceptions to the rule" – perhaps special orders or else the work of particular decorators who wished to stamp their individuality on their work.

Dating mottowares is more difficult because the same styles were used for many years. Pottery backstamps are reasonably accurate although some former pottery workers have said that when they were really busy they often used old stamps that had not seen the light of day for years. Early cottagewares often had very elaborate borders with coloured bands, seaweed decoration and scrolls; on later wares borders were greatly reduced, or even aban-

doned altogether on some items made in the 1950's and 1960's. Long mottoes are also another indication of early products, although Dartmouth used some transfers of long mottoes on puzzle jugs in the 1960's. Transfer printed place names were used on some Watcombe pottery shortly before the pottery closed in 1962. Glazes can also be used to date the pottery, early glazes often being slightly yellow due to the lead in them. After World War II lead was banned for health reasons (death from lead poisoning was fairly common in the pottery industry) and the new glazes were more transparent so the cream slip ground colour appears white and the colours brighter. In the mid 1950's Watcombe experimented with cottagewares done in contemporary shades of lime green, turquoise and tan; presumably these were not very popular as they are rarely seen today.

Fig. 15 Longpark bottle vase 7" (18 cms) tall with faience painting of a cottage. Neck and lower half of pot is painted in beige.

Fig. 16 Three timber ended cottages. Left, jardiniere made of white clay with brown slip applied to interior, late Crown Dorset; plate by the Plymouth Pottery; Honiton Art Pottery jug.

# Crown Dorset

Faience cottages from c. 1906, slip cottages from c. 1912, although both were done in similar styles.

Cottage outlined in dark brown. Steeply sloping roof of pale brown/yellowy slips.
Usually single storey, often large windows, style varies a lot.
Trees and grass of muddy greens to lighter sage greens, going right round vases, jugs etc.
Path irregular and sometimes winding.
Distinctive rounded sgraffito lettering; Dorset dialect quotations from William Barnes and Thomas Hardy often used.
From 1916–25 the quality of cottagewares declined. Gable ended

cottages very similar to Hart and Moist, or Forster and Hunt; trees crudely done and no path. Clay either orangey red, or white perhaps with brown slip interior.
Lettering usually erratic and poorly executed.

Fig. 17

Fig. 18

# Hart and Moist

c. 1912–c. 1932

Cottage outlined in black slip, windows and doors black slip; roof covering (? thatch) chocolate brown slip.

Trees and grass in shades of green with chocolate brown path leading to cottage.

On bowls, jugs, teapots etc., the greenery completely encircles the pot.

Borders – usually thin band of green.

Lettering – sgraffito, uneven and usually backwards sloping.

Clay often speckled and gritty.

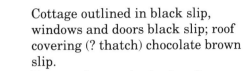

Fig. 19

Fig. 20

# Watcombe

c. 1915–1962

Two story cottage, outlined in sgraffito, roof filled in with brown slips, door usually black.

Sgraffito windows, sometimes divided into four panes in childlike fashion.

Wide path of tan slips, trees and grass mid to dark green.

On jugs, teapots, bowls etc., the scene is confined to the front, only the borders go right round the pot.

Larger items often have two or even three cottages in a row.

Borders vary a lot. Early items have elaborate borders consisting of green and brown scrolls, seaweed design, dots etc., also blue dots and bands. By late 1930's borders much plainer, consisting of a single band or row of blue dots. c. 1960 borders sometimes missing altogether.

Lettering very well formed and neat.

Who burnt the Table cloth

A place for . everything

Fig. 21

# Aller Vale

c. 1915–1924

Aller Vale cottages are not very common. Many are indistinguishable from Watcombe both in terms of style of cottage and lettering; this is because Watcombe and Aller Vale were both owned by Hexter Humpherson and Co. and there was some interchange of personnel so they were probably done by the same decorators. However, some Aller Vale mottowares have a more distinctive cottage with a very angular perspective.

I cum frum Paignton

Fig. 22

# Forster and Hunt, Honiton

c. 1915

Cottage outlined in dark brown/black slip; windows and doors also very dark brown. Roof and chimney mid brown. Trees sparse, and very thin line of greenery which goes right round the pot. Path very thin.

Background colour of pot often pale lemon with sage green or pale blue border.

Sgraffito lettering often poorly formed. Forster and Hunt cottages are rarely found; the style of cottage and lettering, and the shape of the pots are very similar to Hart and Moist suggesting that there was a link between these potteries.

Fig. 23

Fig. 24

# Honiton Art Potteries

c. 1920

Outline of cottage, windows, trees, hedge all piped in dark brown slip as "tube lining". Exposed timbers sometimes shown on end wall, also tube lined.

Roof brown; roof of "extension" (if there is one) often in blue. Trees seagreen, sometimes mustard; hedges in seagreen go right round pot. Sgraffito lettering erratic.

Honiton Art pottery cottages were only made for two or three years and are rarely found. They are similar to Crown Dorset as both potteries were owned by Charles Collard.

Fig. 25

# Plymouth Pottery

c. 1926–1928

Cottages outlined in black slip,
windows and doors also black slip;
exposed timbers on end wall.
Roof and chimney mid brown slip.
Trees and hedgerows sparse but go
right round the pot; path very thin.
Background sky behind the cottage is
usually yellow with turquoisy-blue
above. Borders usually dark green.
Sgraffito lettering often slightly
angular and backwards sloping.
Clay usually very red with slight
specks of black.
Plymouth Pottery cottages are similar
to Hart and Moist, and Forster and
Hunt, however, the sky is much
deeper in colour on Plymouth pots.

East or West. Homes best.

Fig. 26

# Timber Framed Cottages – a comparison

Several smaller potteries made timber framed cottages. Because there are not many to be found collectors may find it helpful to see examples grouped together for the purpose of comparison and identification.

Fig. 27 Left to right, top row: Crown Dorset c. 1920; Plymouth Pottery Co.; Torquay Pottery Co., Hele Cross – this cottage has been decorated in pigments. Bottom row: Hart and Moist, Exeter; Honiton Art Potteries.

# Longpark

c. 1920–1957

Typically a single storey cottage outlined in sgraffito with chocolate brown slip roof. Black slip door and chimney.
Well defined windows usually divided into four panes.
Trees and hedgerows in shades of green go completely round pots. Broad path in brown or tan slip.
Borders of "commas" or dots, or plain bands in green or blue around rims and bases of pots.
All sgraffito work done with broad, flat based tool.
Lettering distinctive, often with curly letter "e" – a speciality of motto writers Len Mayo and Sid Bond.
Clay often very dark chocolate brown.

A place for Ashes

Fig. 28

# Torquay Pottery Company

c. 1920–1939

Torquay Pottery made two distinct styles of slip decorated cottagewares:

1. Sgraffito outlines very much in the style of those at the Watcombe Pottery; lettering usually more erratic and thicker than Watcombe, and items 'chunky' and more heavily potted.

2. Very thin sgraffito outline, with thick brown slip roof to represent thatch. Sgraffito windows indistinct. Trees and hedgerows sparse. Short sgraffito motto or place name; sometimes no motto at all. These cottages are usually of poor quality; frequently there is a very deep royal blue band around the base of the pot, occasionally a tan or green band.

Fig. 29

# Devon Tors

c. late 1920's–1950's.

Cottage outline done in sgraffito using a fine needle.

Roof overhangs cottage and is thick to represent thatch; done in brown slip with black chimneys.

Windows sgraffito but poorly formed and indistinct; occasionally windows have blue slip infill. Doors black.

Surrounding trees in dark green, on larger items there is often a lot of detailing. Grass usually bright or lime green.

Scene painted on front of item only. Usually there are borders of large bright blue dots, and deep bands of bright blue slip – the colour was called lapis lazuli and is quite distinctive.

Sgraffito letters done in large, clear, upright characters, or sometimes "running writing".

Base of pots either glazed or dry based; when glazed they have a slightly "greasy" look.

Fig. 30

# Dartmouth

1.

Sgraffito and slip cottage.

2.

Slip cottage.

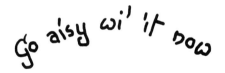

c. 1948–1960's

Dartmouth developed two distinct styles of cottage:

1. 1948 – early 1950's: sgraffito outlined two storey cottages very much in the style of Watcombe. Small blue slip dots sparsely positioned around rims; sometimes also thin blue borders. Lettering thinner and more rounded than Watcombe; mottoes usually short.

2. Early 1950's onwards: Squat slip decorated cottage. Roof outlined in black with thick tan slip 'thatch'. Tan/black door. Very distinctive blue slip dots for windows. Trees, hedgerows, grass in shades of green on front of pot only. Tan path, often curved. Overall, a poorly decorated cottage. This type of cottage was also used on later slip cast wares made of white clay – on these, the mottoes were usually painted in brown pigment or transfer printed.

Fig. 31

Fig. 32

# Babbacombe

1952 – early 1960's

Cottage outlined in sgraffito; steeply pitched roof usually of two shades of brown to give shadow effect. Black chimneys and door. Indistinct sgraffito windows.
Cottage often has an extension at side or back (or both).
Trees, hedgerows, grass of olive, or grey-green colour. Very broad path.
Scene is painted only on front of pot.
Often two 'birds' in sky to right of cottage (birds also appear on some Devon Tors and Devonshire Potteries wares).
Usually a thin blue line drawn around the pot under the cottage scene.
Sgraffito lettering in distinctive rounded characters.
Generally a well decorated cottage with good quality glazes.

Vessels

Venture more

The Lizard

Fig. 33

Fig. 34 Selection of slip decorated cottagewares from the smaller potteries. Top row, left to right: Devon Tors mugs; Crown Dorset watering jug; Plymouth Pottery jug. Bottom row: small vase with deep blue band at base by Torquay Pottery Co.; Hart and Moist ashtray; Torquay Pottery candlestick; Honiton Pottery teapot.

# St. Marychurch

1962–1969

Cottages done in sgraffito in style of
Watcombe.
Windows clearly drawn and usually in
two or four panes; outline of windows
often slightly curved.
Sgraffito letters are rounded and
slightly erratic.

Fig. 35.

Looe

Dounee hurry daunce scur

# Cyril Wilson Wares

c. 1989 onwards

Identical to St. Marychurch as Cyril
Wilson was part owner of that pottery.

# Devonshire Potteries

c. 1948–late 1950's

Sgraffito and slip cottages very much in the style of Watcombe, often two 'birds' in sky to right of cottage. These cottagewares are rarely seen.

# Ron Jackson Wares

c. 1989 onwards

Cottages vary a lot in style.
Colours pale and muted, often blue infill to sgraffito windows.
Borders usually of brown scrolls.
Sgraffito mottoes usually in imitation of handwriting.

Fig. 36 Some of the later Torquay cottagewares. Left to right, top row: St. Marychurch plate; Babbacombe jug and bell; Ron Jackson plate. Bottom row: St. Marychurch beaker and ashtray; Babbacombe jug; Ron Jackson mug.

# Individual Decorators

THE Torquay potteries each had their own style of cottage and decorators were given drawings to copy – thus, the potteries positively discouraged individuality. So although the names of some decorators are known, it is almost impossible to put those names to particular pots. There are, however, a few exceptions. In spite of the potteries uniform approach, one or two decorators still managed to stamp their individuality on the pots they decorated, the most well known of these being Harry Crute.

Harry Edmunds Crute was born in Torquay in 1888 and gained employment in several of the local potteries. Before the Great War he was working at the Torquay Pottery Company at Hele Cross, then in 1914 he went into part-

Fig. 37 Watcombe fruit bowl beautifully decorated by Harry Crute with two cottages. The motto on the reverse is "God be thanked for this here banquet which we have had together, Give us grace to work apace so we may earn another".

nership with Tom Lemon, a thrower from North Devon, and they both took a lease on the Tor Vale pottery in Teignmouth Road. The Lemon & Crute partnership lasted until 1926. During this time they produced some high quality art pottery but do not appear to have made any cottagewares, except, perhaps, a few pieces decorated with individual named cottages. In 1926 Tom Lemon went to Weston super Mare to start a new pottery leaving Harry Crute to run the old pottery on his own account as the Daison Art pottery. Most Daison wares were very similar to Lemon & Crute. The Daison Pottery suffered badly in the Depression and went into liquidation in the autumn of 1931.

By 1935 Harry Crute was working at the Watcombe pottery and it was during this time that he developed his own particular style of cottage with an inglenook fireplace. Harry Crute was

Fig. 38 Longpark advertising shop stand 3½" (9cms) tall. Made c. 1950 from a Watcombe mould.

Fig. 39 Watcombe plate showing an individual style cottage set beside a field bounded by a fence; 8" (20 cms) diameter.

an accomplished artist specialising in local views; for many years he sold small land and seascapes through Boots the Chemists. Torre Abbey Museum in Torquay has a large watercolour by Harry Crute which depicts a cottage with an inglenook fireplace. Collectors should look out for these paintings at sales as the Devon views form an appropriate background to a collection of Harry Crute cottagewares. The paintings are usually signed, or initialled HEC in the corner. It has sometimes been said that the prototype drawings for cottagewares were taken from real cottages; this has not yet been proven and even Harry Crute's cottage paintings are usually titled "Devon Cottage" etc., rather than attributed to any particular cottage.

In addition to decorating thousands of pieces of mottoware at Watcombe, Harry Crute also designed the company's advertising shopstand (fig. 40).

This is 3½" tall and is modelled in relief with a typical Crute cottage surrounded by a profusion of flowers against a backdrop of trees; the decoration is done in pigments, not slip, which gives finer detailing. After World War II, Watcombe pottery bought out the Longpark pottery and the shopstand was adapted to advertise their wares even though no Longpark pottery has been seen depicting this style of cottage (see fig. 38). Some of the advertising stands are inscribed "Royal Watcombe Pottery, Devon Motto Ware, Torquay" whilst others have "England" instead of "Torquay". It is believed those inscribed "England" were intended for overseas outlets. Harry Crute also painted some faience style cottages while at Watcombe but these are rarely found today.

In 1948 a new pottery was opened at Dartmouth to produce mottowares and similar pottery in Torquay styles; Harry Crute was soon recruited as their chief decorator, and many early Dartmouth cottages are virtually identical to his work at Watcombe. The Dart-

Fig. 40 Selection of slip decorated pots by Harry Crute. The "Widecombe" jug was made at Dartmouth, the rest are Watcombe.

Fig. 41 Two handled loving cup decorated with two cottages and inscribed with "God speed the plough" verse. Made by Watcombe, late 1930s, decorated by Harry Crute.

Fig. 42 Watcombe faience jug decorated by Harry Crute – a very late faience item dating from the mid 1930s.

mouth Pottery presumably valued his skills because they allowed him to sign some of his work although, so far, none of his cottagewares have been seen bearing his signature. Harry Crute died in 1976 at the age of 87 – a pity he didn't live just a few more years to see the appreciation of Torquay pottery which began modestly in the mid 1970's.

Another style of cottage which is quite distinctive is that with a gable over the front door, mid way along the roof (see fig. 43). This is believed to be the design of Bill Critchlow who worked at Watcombe from the 1930's up until the pottery closed. Very little is known about his artistic career, although since he was employed as a decorator for many years he obviously became a skilled worker who produced many thousands of cottageware pots.

There is still much research to be done on individual decorators and collectors can contribute to this by examining their own cottagewares for similarities of style. Fig. 47 illustrates two late mottoware pots depicting similar cottages. On the left is a Babba-

Fig. 43 Selection of Watcombe pots decorated by Bill Critchlow.

Fig. 44 Puzzle jug with cottage decorated in the Bill Critchlow style with a gable half way along the front. Watcombe.

Fig. 45 Watcombe biscuit barrel, decorated by Bill Critchlow c. 1930.

Fig. 46 Watcombe giant sized teapot to hold 8 pints decorated with cottages under an amber glaze c. 1930. These were often placed in the windows of teashops to advertise Devon cream teas.

Fig. 47 Left: Babbacombe jug; right: Dartmouth mug. Note the similarity in style of cottage and windows—they are believed to have been decorated by Peter Priddoe.

Fig. 48 "Help yourself to the cheese and biscuits". Watcombe trefoil dish, Watcombe cheese dish and an unmarked biscuit barrel made by the Torquay Pottery Company. All made in the 1930s.

combe jug and a Dartmouth mug on the right, both dating from the 1950's. The cottages both have similar single storey extensions on the back, chimneys at both ends of the roof, and the indistinct windows all lack a frame at the bottom. These are believed to be the work of Peter Priddoe, who later established a studio pottery at Paignton.

Decorating pots with identical cottages for hours on end every day must have been tedious and one can sympathise with the potters desire to do something different occasionally. Perhaps this explains the "oddities" that occur from time to time such as the plate shown in fig. 39 where the cottage appears to be standing in a field surrounded by grass and a low fence, or the trefoil dish in fig. 48 where one of the bowls has a cottage with a hedge and picket fence with a gate.

Fig. 49 Torquay Pottery tile made of white clay with pigment decorated view described as "Old Uncle Tom Cobleigh's Cottage, Widecombe". The church tower is based on Widecombe Church (known as the Cathedral of the Moors because of its tall granite tower) but Uncle Tom Cobleigh's cottage is fictitious.

Fig. 50 Unusual cottages: Watcombe jug with street scene; Babbacombe cottage converted to a pub by the addition of a hanging sign; Watcombe vase with cottage peeping out behind a windmill.

# Individual Cottages

THE faience ware rural scenes, mottowares and moulded cottages all depict stylised anonymous cottages. However, the potteries also produced particular named cottages, presumably to sell as souvenir wares, and a selection of these is shown in fig. 52. Some of the cottages, such as Anne Hathaway's at Stratford on Avon are very common, whereas others such as the First and Last House at Land's End are rarely seen.

The decoration on faience wares is finely painted which was particularly suitable for named places. The Longpark Pottery specialised in named views, mostly town and street scenes, churches, etc., but they also included a few cottages such as those at Cockington village, near Torquay. Watcombe also produced named cottages in faience ware and those seen include Crazy Kate's cottage at Clovelly, Rose cottage at Coffinswell, Torquay, old cottages at Paignton and the Umbrella cottage at Lyme Regis – a late example made in the 1930's. The Torquay Pottery favoured pigment decoration over relief moulded views of buildings – these are often rather heavily potted and poorly decorated although the First and Last House is an exception.

The Watcombe Pottery decorated a number of pots with slip painted views of named cottages. An early example is Burns Cottage done on a barrel shaped jug. Anne Hathaway's Cottage and Shakespeare's House were always popular; early examples were done in faience style but after World War II the pottery brought out new versions in

Fig. 51 Longpark vase, 5" (12 cms) tall, decorated in pigments with a view of "Rose Cottage" – probably the one in Coffinswell near Torquay.

Fig. 52 Selection of items decorated with individual cottages. Left to right: Burns Cottage decorated in slips at the Watcombe Pottery; Fruit bowl with Anne Hathaway's Cottage and Ashtray with Old Mother Hubbard's Cottage at Yealmpton, Plymouth – both decorated in bright contemporary coloured slips at Watcombe; Vase decorated faience style with Cottages at Cockington Village by Longpark; squat Jug modelled in relief with the First and Last House at Land's End and painted in pigments – Torquay Pottery Company; Watcombe barrel shaped Jug decorated faience style with the Umbrella Cottage at Lyme Regis.

bright coloured slips – they must have sold well as they are quite common today. Much rarer is the very late ashtray depicting Old Mother Hubbard's Cottage at Yealmton, near Plymouth.

Sometimes collectors may come across unnamed cottages which are so individual they must be of a particular place. One such example is shown in fig. 50 – however, unless someone recognises where it is (or was) it remains a mystery.

# Advertising and Commemorative Cottages

**W**ITH the popularity of cottage-wares it was perhaps inevitable that some customers would choose to have this decoration on their own personal commemoratives or advertising wares. These items are not very common, and indeed some are unique "one-off" pots, but they add interest to a collection of mottowares. The potteries were a major tourist attraction for visitors to Devon and sometimes in the 1920's and 30's it was a common sight to see six or seven "charas" lined up in the drive at Longpark. Visitors were encouraged to buy pots from the showroom or to order their own personal souvenirs which could be ready inside a week. Occasionally visitors inscribed, or even decorated, their own pots – collectors can usually recognise these instantly as motto writing was lot harder than it looked!

Some of the earliest cottageware advertising items must be the jugs made by Crown Dorset to advertise Whitbreads Ales; they date from c.1914 (fig. 53). The slip decorated cottage has been "converted" to a pub by having Whitbreads Ales written across the front wall; on the reverse is the motto

In summer's heat
In winter's gales
Naught is so sweet
As Whitbread's Ales

Other adaptations of cottages include the addition of smoke issuing from the chimney on a Watcombe ashtray advertising the Woodfibre Wallboard Company made in the 1930's, and a radio aerial attached to the roof of a cottage on a smaller Watcombe ashtray made to commemorate the Radio Society of Great Britain's Convention at Bristol in September 1954 (fig. 55).

More frequently, standard cottage-wares were converted to advertising or commemorative wares simply by the addition of an appropriate inscription – some of these are shown in figs. 53 and 55. Advertising wares that have been seen so far are:

Hylton Court Hotel, Torquay – Watcombe ashtrays

A. E. Knight & Son, Ironmongers – Longpark ashtrays

Devon Coast Country Club – Dartmouth mugs and ashtrays

Fig. 53 Advertising cottagewares. Left to right, top shelf: Jug made by Crown Dorset to advertise Whitbreads Ales; Dartmouth Mug with transfer printed "Devon Coast Country Club", Bottom row: Longpark ashtray advertising "A. E. Knight & Son, Ironmongers"; Watcombe ashtray to advertise the Wood Fibre Wallboard Company – note the smoke issuing from the chimney; small rectangular ashtray made by Watcombe for the Hylton Court Hotel, Torquay.

The oldest chemist shop,
Knaresborough – Watcombe mugs
and bowls; Babbacombe egg cups

Soyer & Son (butchers/fish shop at
Yeovil) – Longpark ashtrays

G. J. Grose, Slades Stores, St.
Austell, – 1956 Watcombe cream
jugs

The Old Smithy – St. Marychurch
sugar bowls

Conway Nurseries – Babbacombe
ashtrays

Medina Court Hotel, Torquay –
Watcombe ashtrays.

Fig. 54 Devon Tors teapot, 7" (18cms) tall overall, moulded as a round cottage and inscribed "NAHS 1935". Newton Abbot hospital organized a range of festivities every June to raise funds; activities took place over a week culminating in a big carnival on the Saturday, which was known as Newton Abbot Hospital Saturday (NAHS) This teapot was probably made as a prize in one of the competitions, and is a very rare commemorative.

Commemoratives are much more varied because many of them are personal and were made as gifts, for instance a Watcombe cup inscribed "Edna from Leslie and Elsie Xmas 1930", or a Watcombe biscuit barrel "To Kathleen wishing you a very happy birthday June 25th 1953". A Devon Tors mug was made for C. H. Staddon on his 80th birthday (fig. 55) – he was a relative of Enoch "Nocky" Staddon who was a director of the Torquay Pottery Company.

So far only one type of Royal Commemorative has been seen decorated with cottages – these were cream bowls made to commemorate the coronation of May 1937 and an advertisement for the Priory Farm Dairy at Taunton whose name is inscribed on the base. Presumably they were given or sold to

Fig. 55 Commemorative cottagewares. Top row: two personalised commemoratives, mug inscribed "C. H. Staddon 80 Today" made by Devon Tors, cup and saucer "Edna From Leslie and Elsie Xmas 1930" made by Watcombe. Bottom row: cream bowl to commemorate the Coronation in May 1937, also inscribed on the base to advertise "Priory Farm Dairy, Taunton; two Watcombe ashtrays for the 'National Convention Torquay 1952" and the Radio Society of Great Britain's Convention at Bristol in September 1954. Note the radio aerial on the RSGB ashtray; Radio Society members unable to attend the Convention could buy the ashtrays from the Secretary for 3/6 (17½p)

customers by the dairy. More commemoratives were made for conferences etc:

National Convention Torquay 1952
  – Watcombe ashtrays

Newquay Conference 1956 –
  Watcombe ashtrays

George Beech Lodge 1902–1952 –
  Watcombe ashtrays

# Moulded Cottagewares

COTTAGE mottowares enjoyed great popularity but the Torquay Pottery Company and Devon Tors also made tablewares *moulded* in the form of a cottage; these are much rarer than mottowares but are becoming increasingly popular with collectors.

The earliest reference to moulded cottagewares occurs in a novel by Eden Phillpotts called "Brunels Tower", published in 1915, which was set in the Torquay Potteries; it describes how Miss Medway, one of the characters, decorated the models:

"The famous 'Devon Cot' was a little model two inches high and two inches long. It resembled a tiny abode, with thatched roof and whitewashed walls, about which climbed honeysuckle and roses. The trifle proved a very popular keepsake among the thousands of visitors who annually came from the north for holidays in summertime. Miss Medway enjoyed painting the 'Devon Cot'. It was a labour of love to set in the little blue windows, spread 'orange-gold' over the thatch, paint the chimney red, and with

delicate brushes trailed the creepers over the whitewashed face of it".

Brunels Tower refers to the Longpark Pottery which occupied buildings which had formerly been part of Brunel's atmospheric railway scheme; however, many of the decorations and techniques described were peculiar to other Torquay potteries so it can be assumed that "Brunels Tower" is an amalgam of all the potteries. No models of cottages have been seen which were made at Longpark, and the description of Miss Medway's cottage exactly fits the Torquay Pottery Company's model so they must surely be one and the same (see fig. 58).

It is not known whether the Torquay Pottery Company made any other moulded wares as early as c.1915; the company rarely advertised, and a photograph of their stand at the British Industries Fair in 1924 does not appear to contain any moulded cottages. The Torquay Pottery Company went into receivership in November 1931 with liabilities of nearly £4,000, yet in spite of this the following April the same directors established a new Company called

Fig. 56 Moulded cottagewares. Small jug by Devon Tors, plate and pint mug by Torquay Pottery Co. The grass around the base of Devon Tors pots is both darker green and deeper than their Torquay Pottery counterparts.

Fig. 57 Moulded cottagewares. Condiments by Devon Tors, teapot and jampot by the Torquay Pottery.

Fig. 58 Little model of a cottage made by the Torquay Pottery Company. It exactly fits the description of the little cottage painted by Miss Medway in Brunel's Tower by Eden Phillpotts.

Torquay Pottery (1932) Ltd. (well before the creditors had received a penny from the previous company!). The new company's notepaper included drawings of their popular lines which showed moulded cottage wares.

Some of the Torquay Pottery's moulded cottages, which they described as "real Devon Cottage Ware", are shown in figs. 56, 57 and 59. They made teapots, coffee pots and jugs in different versions – the spouts and handles show variations. Also there were sugar bowls and jampots in different sizes, biscuit barrels, toast racks, cheese dishes and muffin dishes. Cups and saucers, tea plates and bread plates were also produced (although they are hard to find) so customers could make up teasets if they wished. A few ashtrays were produced

too, which had a flat rectangular base with a small model of a cottage to one side. Plus, of course, the little models of a cottage. From advertisements, these seem to have been made in three versions yet they are rarely seen today; the models were probably originally made as children's toys so no doubt many would have got broken.

Some moulded cottagewares in the Torquay style are marked on the base "Bovey Tracey Art Pottery" – this pottery was a subsidiary of the Torquay Pottery Company and their wares are identical. Collectors should be careful not to confuse the Bovey Tracey Art Pottery with Devon Tors which was also at Bovey Tracey.

The Devon Tors Pottery was a small company established after World War I by Robert Fry, William Bond and Frank Bond (brothers). They made similar wares to the Torquay Pottery including mottowares and moulded cottage wares. Devon Tors moulded cottages are more finely modelled and less chunky than their Torquay counterparts; the colours are brighter too and the Devon Tors blue (which they called Lapis Lazuli) is a quite distinctive shade. Devon Tors pots typically have a deep dark green band of "grass" around the base whereas on Torquay pots the "grass" is narrower, often patchy, and in pale green.

Moulded cottagewares do not have mottoes although some have place names inscribed in black paint. A few teapots made by the Torquay Pottery are attributed as "Old Uncle Tom Cobley's Cottage" – this is a fictitious building, although the house in Widecombe in the Moor which houses Uncle Tom Cobley's Chair is made of Dartmoor stone and slate, nothing like the pottery teapots.

Fig. 59 Advertising feature in the Pottery Gazette, June 1938, showing the Torquay Pottery's range of Devon Cottage Ware which "typifies the peaceful happiness of that famous county".

POTTERY GAZETTE AND GLASS TRADE REVIEW, FEBRUARY, 1958

Ann Hathaway's Cottage
Stratford-on-Avon.

ONE
OF
OUR
FOURTEEN
CELEBRATED
MINIATURE
COTTAGES

*Manufacturers of Ornamental
Pottery
Mugs, Beakers and
Breakfast
Sets*

The Devonmoor Art Pottery Ltd.

LIVERTON
NEWTON ABBOT
ENGLAND

———

*Northern Agents :*
ROGER FRANK CURTIS (NORWICH) LTD
90 PRINCE OF WALES ROAD
NORWICH
TELEPHONE 27320

TELEPHONE BICKINGTON 219

Fig. 60 Cigarette box in the form of Anne Hathaway's Cottage made by the Devonmoor Pottery, 1930s.

Fig. 61 TV set which became popular in the mid 1950s. This has a rimless plate which was an American fashion. Watcombe.

# The Range of Wares Produced

BY the early twentieth century mottowares had become established as popular lines in the South Devon potteries. An article in the Pottery Gazette of December 1906 described the products of Hart & Moist:

"Mottoware is a very conspicuous section of their production, and several new and quaint inscriptions have been added to the already large selection". Therefore, when the new slip painted cottage decorations were introduced c.1912 it was relatively simple to adapt the same range to the new pattern.

The most popular items sold were tablewares such as teapots, jugs, bowls and plates, etc., and these remained dominant for over fifty years. Most domestic items were made in different shapes and sizes too, for instance a Watcombe catalogue from the mid 1930's illustrates four different shapes of teapot and each shape was made in four sizes; the most popular teapot was a short squat angular pot with the shape number 1476 (see fig. 62). In addition to the four standard sizes the 1476 was made as part of dolls teasets and also in a giant 8 pint size which was often used as an advertisement. Although the standard teapots are quite common today, the miniature and giant teapots are highly sought by collectors and command high prices.

Other popular early cottagewares include candlesticks and holders in many styles, tobacco jars, shaving mugs, inkwells, pen trays, matchstrikers and hatpin holders – as fashions and social habits changed so there

Fig. 62 Watcombe teapot in the 1476 shape. This was the most popular teapot shape; it was made by virtually all the Torquay potteries and was produced for fifty years. Watcombe advertised four standard sizes in their catalogues, but miniature and giant versions were also made. This one is a large standard size to hold two pints.

Fig. 63 For ladies and gentlemen's toilette. Left to right, top row: Longpark shaving mug; hatpin holder and shaving mug by Watcombe. Bottom row: Watcombe Aladdin's lamp candle holder; candlestick, powder bowl and hair pin tray by Longpark.

was less demand for these items and the post war catalogues do not show them at all, consequently there are fewer around today. However, new lifestyles brought forth new lines in cottagewares such as an electric lamp base and a "TV set", both introduced in the 1950's. The TV set (fig. 61) consisted of a plate with its own attached saucer and cup at one end. Similar items had been made by many Staffordshire potteries in the Victorian period when they were known as croquet sets; in the 1920's they were revived as Tennis sets and in the 1950's they were TV sets, thus reflecting changing leisure pursuits. The Watcombe TV sets had a rimless plate

which was a new innovation in the 1950's, an idea imported from the USA. Critics in Britain claimed they would not catch on because there was "nowhere to put the salt" – perhaps this explains why they are rarely found today.

Collectors always like to look for unusual items to add to their collections and those which are eagerly sought today include biscuit barrels, udder vases, dog bowls, fish shaped ashtrays, puzzle jugs, large dressing table trays and toast racks – even rarer are the novelty items such as the Watcombe model of a Cornish Pasty, the Torquay Pottery Company's lemon squeezer, and the models of bells made by Babbacombe and Dartmouth.

Old catalogues are valuable because they show the range of standard wares and also the wholesale prices. A Watcombe catalogue c.1935 illustrates 95 different items some of which were made in up to six sizes. It is also interesting to compare prices for the same item at different periods. Trefoil dishes, such as is shown in fig. 48, sold for 24/- (£1.20) a dozen in 1935, in 1957 they had gone up to 81/6 (£4.08) a dozen and the cottage decoration was only applied to one of the bowls, the others being decorated with trees and the motto. The most expensive items in the 1935 catalogue were 8″ diameter porridge tureens with lids which sold for 48/- (£2.40) a dozen; the cheapest were the squat egg "tubs" at 5/- (25p) a dozen.

The Watcombe Pottery produced the widest range of items which is not surprising since they were in operation the longest. Longpark produced a varied range but they are much less common than Watcombe. The Longpark Pottery made a lot of mottowares decorated with cockerels or the scandy pattern, but cottagewares seem to have been almost a sideline until after World War II; a catalogue from the 1930's does not illustrate the design at all! Dartmouth and Babbacombe potteries were established after World War II and manufactured a lot of cottagewares although there is less variety and tablewares predominate.

Mottowares were going out of fashion by the mid 1950's which forced the few surviving companies to diversify or face financial ruin. Longpark never really recovered from wartime restrictions and went out of business in 1957. The Watcombe Pottery tried to give cottagewares wider appeal by decorating them in brighter "contemporary" colours; they also introduced a new "winter cottage" on a blue ground showing the cottage with snow on its roof surrounded by fir trees also covered in snow (see fig. 66). This decoration is hard to find but is popular with collectors today even though it is relatively recent. In spite of diversification, Watcombe went out of business in 1962; Dartmouth and Babbacombe stopped making hand thrown wares altogether and concentrated on cheaper slipcast wares which they still produce in the 1990's.

Fig. 64 Three common tablewares from the Watcombe Pottery.

Fig. 65 Candleholder and mug by Watcombe.

Fig. 66 From a Watcombe catalogue c. 1958 showing some of their range of Winter Cottage ware on a blue ground. The design was introduced in 1957.

WINTER COTTAGE WARE

(ON BLUE BACKGROUND)

AVAILABLE IN COMPLETE DEVON MOTTO WARE RANGE

# "New and Quaint Inscriptions"

**M**UCH of the appeal of motto-wares were the mottoes themselves – they added individuality to an otherwise monotonous pot. The potteries continually vied with each other to satisfy the public demand for quaint old time mottoes, old country sayings, dialect quotations or even current catch-phrases. The Pottery Gazette of May 1917 was eloquent in its praise of Watcombe mottoware:

"... the wording is well chosen, whether it be pithy and humorous sayings, racy of the soil, or proverbs or verses calculated to supply a word in season of encouragement and inspiration; and it is invariably set out in clear and plain characters, easy to be read".

Some of the early mottoes had a strong moral or religious tone as on a Watcombe jardiniere:

Life is mostly froth and bubble
Two things stand as stone
Kindness in another's trouble
Courage in your own

or the shorter "Home the spot on earth supremely blest" by Hart & Moist.

Many were quotations from famous authors such as Shakespeare's "Brevity is the soul of wit" or the longer Robbie Burns's saying which was popular on porridge bowls:

Some hae meat and canna eat
An some wad eat that want it
But we hae meat and we can eat
Sae let the Lord be thank it.

Mottowares had a long history in Britain and some of these were copied by the Torquay potteries; one example is the popular verse which was used on a Bristol delftware puzzle jug made in the eighteenth century:

From mother earth I take my Birth
Am made a joke for man
And now am here fill'd with good
 cheer
Come taste it if you can

In other instances, new mottoes were created to suit changing customs such as the Watcombe motto:

"Many a (batchelor) ship has been
 wrecked on a permanent wave"

which dates from the late 1930's. Often old sayings were adapted to bring them

Fig. 67 Watcombe porridge bowl with Robbie Burns motto.

up to date as in "A car on the road is worth two in the ditch".

In addition to mottoes, many pots were also inscribed with the name of a town or tourist spot, to be sold as holiday souvenirs. All the potteries employed salesmen whose jobs were to travel round the country seeking such orders and the diversity of place names is evidence of their success. Naturally south coast resorts are the most common but places as far apart as Gretna Green, Lindisfarne, Mablethorpe and Caernarvon figure prominently too. The potteries also exported widely, mainly to the old colonies and the USA, and many of these wares are inscribed with place names; for instance nearly 50 different Canadian place names have been recorded so far and no

doubt there are many more – overseas collectors should look out for them.

All the mottoes which are recorded in this book have been seen on cottagewares. Although they are attributed to particular potteries, they are by no means exclusive to that pottery as the potteries all copied each other.

# Building a Collection – ideas and suggestions

COTTAGEWARE enthusiasts usually start their collections by buying everything in sight – even yet another sugar bowl or cream jug is lovingly stroked, chips or cracks being over-looked at the delight in finding a treasure to add to the collection. However, as the shelves begin to fill up with more and more pots, the collector slowly realises that the shelves are be-ginning to look more like the showroom at the pottery and "something must be done". The collection needs direction and shape – its time to take stock and do some serious thinking.

A collection is a very personal thing being based on one's individual preferences, space available, colour schemes, and money. Yet, there are still basic themes which enthusiasts might like to consider before deciding how their collections should develop; some ideas and suggestions are offered below.

## Collections based on one pottery

Some collections are based on just one of the manufacturers and collectors seek to build up representative examples of all their cottagewares. The most prolific pottery was Watcombe, although Long-park, Torquay Pottery Company, Dart-mouth and Babbacombe all produced a lot of cottagewares and these are easy to find. There is less variety in the output of the later potteries (Dartmouth and Babbacombe) but Babbacombe in par-ticular made some high quality motto-wares. At the other end of the spectrum, F. H. Honiton and Plymouth Pottery Company made so few cottagewares that they are difficult to find and a col-lection based on these would be very small indeed.

Fig. 68 shows a small collection of Longpark cottagewares; the covered butterdish is unusual because it has the cottage decoration on both the dish and the cover. Longpark cottages are usually single storey, but the small jug is the exception to the rule and shows there are no "absolute rules". Perhaps this was done by a decorator who had recently come from another pottery and had not yet become accustomed to the Longpark house style.

A varied selection of Torquay Pot-tery cottages is shown in fig. 69. Here,

Fig. 68 Selection of slip decorated cottagewares made by the Longpark Pottery. Longpark cottages are usually single storey although the small jug at the front has a double storey cottage.

the items consist of sgraffito cottages, faience cottages, and some decorated entirely in slips. The Torquay Pottery was renowned for trying to undercut the other potteries and some pots were fired only once as an economy measure. Consequently, many items are heavily potted and rather rough looking – indeed, many collectors turn their noses up at "Royal Torquay" as being too inferior to even bother considering. Yet it is very much a case of "give a dog a bad name..." (as the motto says) because not all the products of the Torquay Pottery Company are inferior by any means. The vases with handles moulded in the form of flowers are often very well decorated, and the novelty items such as the coal scuttle have a

certain rustic charm. Other novelties that have been seen include boats, wheelbarrows and hats – they were probably originally made as children's souvenirs.

Dartmouth Pottery made two distinct types of cottage, the sgraffito and slip version, and one with blue dot windows; some of these are shown in fig. 71. The plate, muffin dish and shallow cereal bowl are all early items c. 1950. When the Dartmouth Pottery started in 1948 wartime restrictions were still in force which meant that very little pottery could be sold on the home market. Consequently, most of this early Dartmouth cottageware was exported, particularly to the USA and Canada.

Fig. 70 A selection of Watcombe jugs showing some of the great variety of shapes made. The small narrow jug inscribed "Souvenir from Alderney" is unusual in that the handle is on the left; Torquay cottagewares normally had the handle on the right of the decoration.

Fig. 69 Selection of cottagewares made by the Torquay Pottery Company – note the variety of styles. The vase with moulded flower handles and coal scuttle are decorated with pigments; the small round jam dish has a sgraffito and slip cottage while the other cottages are all slip.

Fig. 71 Cottagewares made by the Dartmouth Pot-tery. The plate, muffin or cheese dish and shallow bowl are the earliest (late 1940s early 1950s) and have typical Watcombe style sgraffito and slip cottages. The other three items are all decorated with cottages with blue dot windows but they show a gradual decrease in craftsmanship. The basket is hand thrown in red clay c. 1955, the toast rack is moulded in red clay, early 1960s; puzzle jug is moulded in white clay and has a transfer printed inscription, late 1960s.

## *Collections based on one particular item*

There is enormous scope for collections based on one (or perhaps, two or three) particular items. Many people collect teapots from any potteries and a group of South Devon Teapots would greatly enhance such a collection. Teapots were made in many shapes and styles (from dolls to giant 8 pint pots) so there is plenty to look for. Some collectors like to include a cup and saucer, sugar and milk to make a teaset for one, as shown in fig. 72. Cups and saucers are also another popular area of collecting, so are candlesticks/holders, inkwells, puzzle jugs or even ordinary milk jugs. Fig. 70 shows a collection of six jugs all made by Watcombe pottery; notice the great variety of shapes and sizes. For some unexplained reason, the Torquay potteries put handles on the right hand side of the cottage decoration, however, the "Souvenir from Alderney" in the photograph shows yet another excep-tion. Some other mottoware decor-ations, such as the scandy pattern, the handles were put on the left – but why all the potteries should have adopted the same convention remains a mystery.

If space is at a premium why not consider a collection of eggcups (fig. 73).

These come in three types, those with a saucer, those with a pedestal and short squat versions known as egg tubs in the 1930's and egg tots in the 1950's. In addition, egg stands were made with either four or six holes to take egg cups; some of the six holed stands were sold with four egg cups plus salt and pepper pots. It is rare to find a stand complete with egg cups and/or condiments; collectors should check egg cups carefully to see that they all match and that they fit snugly into the holes. The correct egg cups have a small round stump on the base which fits in the hole; some dealers have replaced lost cups with egg tots which do not fit well at all. Incidentally, the stands with three holes were for condiments sets, not egg cups (see fig. 74).

A collection of ashtrays also requires very little space as it can be displayed on a low table or even in a case on the wall. As smoking is now socially unacceptable many people are turning out their old ashtrays so there are plenty around for the collector to buy. Fig. 75 shows a selection of ashtrays from various potteries in both slip and faience decorations – groups of rectangular and square ashtrays can be most effective in a small display case.

Fig. 76 shows a collection of Watcombe ashtrays, all slip decorated but in various shapes. The fish shaped tray "A pla(i)ce for ashes" is much sought after by collectors today. The shape dates from just before World War I and was described in "Brunels Tower":

"... and Mr. Pitts, during a lighter moment, had made a little dish, or ashtray, in the shape of a flat fish. Upon it were written the words 'A pla(i)ce for everything', and this joke so pleased the public that the fish was wanted quicker than it could be made".

Fig. 72 Teaset for one. Sugar bowl Aller Vale, rest Watcombe.

Left. Fig. 73 Selection of eggcups from many different potteries. Left to right top row: Watcombe winter cottage; Longpark; Babbacombe; Honiton Art Pottery, Watcombe to advertise The oldest chemist shoppe, Knaresborough; Dartmouth; Babbacombe; Devon Tors. Bottom row: Watcombe with cottage drawn on the saucer; Watcombe; Watcombe stand with 6 cups (they sometimes had 4 cups plus salt and pepper); Cyril Wilson (1991); Watcombe, Harry Crute cottage; Watcombe.

Fig. 75 Selection of ashtrays from various potteries. Top row left to right: Watcombe Anne Hathaway's cottage decorated in slips; Watcombe winter cottage; unmarked ashtray with applied cigarette believed to be Torquay Pottery Company. Middle row: Hart & Moist; Watcombe faience ashtray mid 1930s; Watcombe faience Anne Hathaway's cottage c.1915. Bottom row: Watcombe Moorland cottage c.1926; St. Marychurch; Dartmouth with blue transfer printed "Devon Coast Country Club".

Left. Fig. 74 Condiments. Top row left to right: mustard pot and vinegar bottle, St. Marychurch; Watcombe tall vinegar bottle; St. Marychurch salt and pepper. Bottom row: Dartmouth salt; Watcombe stand; Babbacombe salt and pepper.

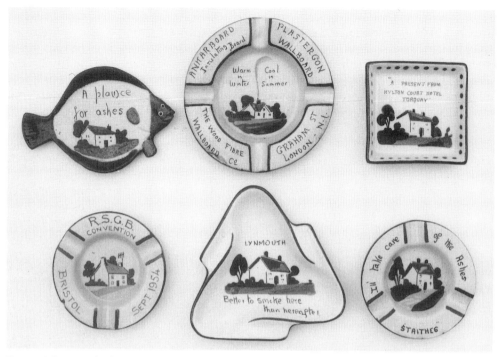

Fig. 76 Selection of ashtrays from the Watcombe Pottery.

This ashtray most probably originated at Longpark and was copied by Watcombe. Mrs. Winifred Anniss who, as Winifred Stockman, worked in the office at Longpark from 1920 to 1930 verified that the visitors really loved the novelty – but also said that the potters wouldn't give them house room because they were just "tourist souvenirs", an attitude probably shared today by many potters making souvenir ware. The fish shaped tray was popular for over twenty years; a Watcombe catalogue of c.1935 advertised them at 7/- (35 pence) a dozen. Collectors should look out for advertising items such as the example inscribed "Soyer and Son Yeovil" – Soyers was a butchers shop but they also sold fish in their earlier days so the "Pla(i)ce for ashes" was a suitable advertising item for their customers.

## Collections based on the mottoes

Much of the appeal of cottagewares was in the mottoes so it is perhaps not surprising that many enthusiasts base their collections on the mottoes too. For some people, mottoes with a religious or devotional theme have particular appeal such as a Watcombe dressing table tray inscribed:

> Work on   Hope on
> Self help is noble schooling
> You do your best and leave the rest
> To God Almighty's ruling

The Pottery Gazette of May 1917 described such verses as "calculated to supply a word in season of encouragement or inspiration". As a general rule "piety pieces" are early, dating from c.1912 to c.1930.

Collectors with an interest in literature might be drawn towards collecting quotations from well known authors, such as Shakespeare, Burns or Thomas Hardy. Most commonly seen are short Shakespearian proverbs such as "Brevity is the soul of wit" or "Neither a borrower nor a lender be", both from Hamlet, which occur on Watcombe and Hart & Moist. Crown Dorset used the less well known couplet:

The friends thou hast and their
    adoption tried
Grapple them to thy heart with
    hoops of steel

which also comes from Hamlet. Another verse which is attributed to Shakespeare is shown in fig. 77:

Piping Pebworth  Dancing Marston,
Haunted Hillbro  Hungry Grafton
Dodging Exhall,  Papist Wixford
Beggarly Broom and Drunken Bidford.

This relates to a story about a drinking spree involving Shakespeare and some of his friends. One Whit Monday the Shakespeare group went to the Falcon pub at Bidford on Avon, seven miles away, for a drinking contest with a group known as the Sippers. Within a short while the Sippers had outdrunk the visitors, who left in a state of drunken humiliation to spend the night under a crabapple tree a mile away. When they awoke next morning, still the worse for drink, Shakespeare is reputed to have declared he would never again drink with men of Piping Pebworth, Dancing Marston... Pebworth, Marston, Hillborough, Grafton, Exhall, Wixford, Broom and Bidford are all villages near Stratford, Pebworth being in Worcestershire, the rest in Warwickshire. Marston was famous for its band of Morris Men who used to go round the local pubs and fairs; Grafton is on a hill and has poor stoney soil; Wixford was

Fig. 77 Watcombe ashtray with Shakespeare verse.

Fig. 78 Selection of items with Welsh inscriptions. Tall jug and bowl with handle both made by Watcombe, other three by Longpark.

dominated by the local Throckmorton family who were Roman Catholics, but why the other villages were given their attributions is largely open to speculation and guesswork. This verse was used by the Watcombe pottery on ashtrays (as shown in the photograph), mugs and jugs. Presumably these were souvenirs intended for sale in the named villages, and perhaps in Stratford on Avon too. A collection of Shakespearian quotations would be enhanced with pots depicting Shakespeare's House and Anne Hathaway's cottage.

On similar lines, a collection could be built up of sayings from Robbie Burns together with pots decorated with views of Burns' cottage. The porridge plate in fig. 67 is inscribed with Burns' quotation known as the Selkirk Grace. Another popular inscription came from the poem "To a Louse":

O wad some Pow'r the giftie gie us
to see oursels as others see us

The Crown Dorset Pottery favoured quotations from local authors such as Thomas Hardy or William Barnes who wrote in local dialect, but these are not very common. No doubt there are quotations from many more sources – unfortunately the Torquay potteries did not normally attribute their mottoes so it would take a keen student of literature to identify them all.

Experts would also be needed to translate the mottoes in foreign languages which appear on many cottagewares. Welsh is the most common, but mottoes in French, Irish, Manx and Maori have been seen with other decorations so perhaps some will turn up on cottagewares too. However, as the motto writers did not understand the language they were inscribing mistakes often occur. It is believed that the shops in Wales which ordered the souvenir wares also sent in the mottoes too. Fig. 78 shows a collection of items inscribed with Welsh mottoes; these are from the Watcombe and Longpark potteries although Dartmouth also did a large trade in Welsh wares too.

For some collectors, their ambition is to try and find long mottoes – this style of collecting particularly appeals to Americans, who also like pots with two or even three cottages as opposed to the more usual single cottage. No doubt the two handled loving cup in fig. 80 would be highly coveted; it has two cottages and is inscribed with the old farmers toast "God speed the plough" which has been used for over two hundred years.

> I eat my own lamb
> My own chickens and ham
> I shear my own fleece and wear it
> So Jolly boys now
> Here's God speed the plough
> Long life and success to the Farmer.

Torquay mottowares were "cheap and cheerful" souvenirs or gifts and were intended to bring a note of cheer or impart a serious message in a humorous way – what recalcitrant letter writer could fail to respond to an inkwell inscribed "Zend us a line, us baint dade". An amusing verse such as

> Up to the lips and over the gums
> Look out tummy here it comes

on a Watcombe beer mug would, no doubt, seem hilarious after a drink or two!

Sometimes the "message" in a motto came from the use of puns or ambiguous word play; examples of these are a Longpark water jug inscribed "Water is alright if taken in the right Spirit", or a Watcombe barrel shaped jug with the warning "Don't give your husband too much rope, he might skip". Any husbands who felt this to be too "sexist" could always respond with an ashtray declaring "Many a man sends his wife

Fig. 79 Longpark shaving mug 4¾" (12 cms) tall with Welsh inscription "Heb dduw heb ddim" (Without God without anything).

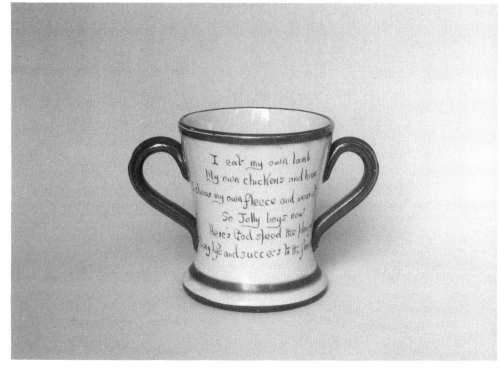

Fig. 80 "God speed the plough" motto on a Watcombe loving cup. Reverse of Fig. 41.

away for a rest because *he* needs it" (fig. 81). One of the most delightful of all humorous verses is one seen on a giant sized Devon Tors teapot (spelling as on the pot):

> Give me a mind that is not bored
> That does not whimper, whine or
>  sigh
> Don't let me worry over much
> About that little thing called I
> Give me a sence of humor Lord
> Give me the grace to see a joke
> To get some happeness from life
> And pass it on to other folk

In addition to mottoes, many pots were also inscribed with the name of a town, and this could form the basis of a collection – perhaps the collector's home town or favourite resort. Some thought must be given to the choice of town though – a collection based on "Torquay" would soon reach unmanageable proportions whereas one based on "St. Albans" would be very small indeed – in fifteen years of collecting the author has found only one example (see fig. 78). The most common place names are, predictably, holiday resorts in South West England, but the scope is enormous from popular Cotswolds tourist spots such as Broadway, to the remote north country village of Stanhope, famous for its fossilised tree. Many pots intended for the export market were inscribed with place names too so overseas collectors should look out for these.

## Decorating with cottagewares

For some enthusiasts, their collections are chosen to fit in with a particular

Fig. 81 Watcombe ashtray and jug with "sexist" mottoes.

decorating scheme in their homes. A collection of Watcombe faience wares with green bands can look most effective when displayed against pale green furnishings, and the fine quality of decoration on plates and trays makes them suitable for grouping as pictures on a wall. The Moorland cottages can be just as attractive in rooms decorated in shades of pink or mauve. Jardinieres can be shown to best advantage if they are *used* (as was originally intended) for pot plants. Choose flowers such as primroses or chrysanthemums because they are more in keeping with the fashion of the time – more exotic plants were not available in those days. A jardiniere decorated with a Moorland cottage would be most suited to a pot of moorland heathers. Always make sure that flower pots have deep saucers to catch the water; if water is allowed to remain in jardinieres (or vases) it may get into cracks in the glaze and seep into the pot.

Eventually this will cause the slip and glaze on the outside of the pot to flake off, the only remedy being to restore and re-fire the pot.

Faience wares are most suited to living rooms, halls or bedrooms, but cottagewares can be used almost anywhere in the home. A collection of domestic wares (tea sets, jugs, etc.) will look homely in the kitchen, or displayed on a pine dresser in the dining room. A word of warning though about displaying pots in the kitchen. If pots are subjected to extreme changes of heat, or to a lot of steam they can crack and sometimes the glaze will flake. Too much grease on a pot will seep into hairline cracks and is impossible to remove – sometimes grease will discover cracks you didn't even know were there. Try grouping tablewares according to their function, such as breakfast items together (see

Fig. 82 Variety of jardinieres – or plant pots as they were then known. Watcombe slip cottageware; small white clay pot made by the Dorset Pottery c 1922; Watcombe faience pot c. 1907. Notice the elaborate borders of bands, dots and "seaweed" on the large jardiniere – this is typical of early cottagewares c. 1925; height 5½" (14cms).

fig. 83 – or set up a small table in a corner as tea for one.

In the living room, or study, a group of writing items can be displayed on a desk (fig. 86 – or a feature made of puzzle jugs, beer mugs, tobacco jars and match strikers. For the bedroom or bathroom, there are items for gentlemen and ladies toilette – shaving mugs, hatpin holders and powder bowls etc. Most effective of all is a complete dressing table set but these are rarely found. The components of sets varied but would normally consist of a dressing table tray, pair of candlesticks, hatpin holder, small oval or rectangular hair pin tray, powder and powder puff bowls, a ring holder and hair tidy; possibly scent bottles might be included too.

## Collections of miniatures and children's ware

Children's wares and miniatures have been a popular area of collecting for many years, partly because the items are small and take up little space, but also because they conjure up nostalgic memories of ones own childhood. Some children's wares are rare and consequently expensive, so are definitely for adults only, but mugs or plates with nursery rhymes are still relatively common and can be given to children to encourage their interest in collecting too. Fig. 85 shows a selection of children's wares and miniatures; two of the little model cottages were made by the Devonmoor Art Pottery at Liverton, near Bovey Tracey. The Pottery started in 1922 and used mainly local white clay, as opposed to brown clay favoured by the Torquay potteries. During the 1920's and 30's they modelled many

Fig. 83 Selection of breakfast wares. Top shelf: three porridge bowls, one on the right by Dartmouth, other two Watcombe. Bottom row: Toast rack on the right unmarked, other two by Watcombe.

Fig. 84 Watcombe dolls teaset. Teapot 3″ (7.5cms) tall.

buildings ranging from a cigarette box in the form of Anne Hathaway's cottage to a series of fourteen miniature cottages. Many were named buildings such as Burns cottage, or Umbrella cottage at Lyme Regis, but others were stylised versions of a typical cottage at Selworthy, or a smuggler's cottage. The cottages are quite charming; they were all hand painted and frequently bear the paintresses initials in black paint on the base. Miniature cottages were made in the post war period too; when the pottery closed in 1977 some former employees acquired the moulds and continued to make the cottages for many years – they are virtually identical to their earlier counterparts although the colours are paler.

Complete dolls teasets are rare and

Fig. 85 Items for children. Top row, left to right: models of Anne Hathaway's cottage and Saxon cottage by the Devonmoor Pottery; thatched cottage by Torquay Pottery Company; jug and basin from a dolls teaset by Watcombe. Bottom row: mugs and a beaker for children by Watcombe. The beaker is inscribed "Simple Simon met a pieman".

highly sought by collectors today (fig. 84). A set usually consisted of teapot, sugar, cream, two cups and saucers; in 1935 these cost 24/- (£1.20) a dozen sets, in 1957 they had gone up to 92/- (£4.60). Some sets also included two plates, and others were sold with a tray. Watcombe placed an advertisement in the Christmas Gifts section of the Pottery Gazette for 1937 – this showed a child's teaset on a rectangular tray, the sort normally sold as a dressing table tray. The teaset was decorated with cockerels, while the tray displayed a typical Bill Critchlow cottage – a "mix and match" set. The mottoes on dolls teasets were usually nursery rhymes such as "Jack & Jill", "Hey diddle diddle" or "Mary had a little lamb". These same mottoes were also used on larger mugs, beakers, and plates that were intended as children's gifts, brought home from holiday by doting grandparents, aunts and parents; some also have children's names, or a date which was probably a birthday or christening.

Fig. 86 "Send us a scrape of yer pen". Items for the desk: faience pen tray by Longpark, Honiton inkwell; Watcombe lamp base decorated in bright contemporary slips; Watcombe inkwell. Postcard from a series which depicted Torquay mottoware cream bowls c. 1915.

Fig. 87 "A pint and a pasty". Left to right, top row: Pint "Ovaltine" shaped mug and puzzle jug by Watcombe; Longpark straight sided mug. Bottom row: Watcombe pasty which is very rare – the motto "Nort but taters" (Nothing but potatoes) is a reference to the hard times which were common in Cornwall when there was no money to buy meat so pasties were filled with just potatoes and herbs; Aller Vale match striker; Watcombe fish shaped ashtray.

Fig. 88 Devon cream tea. Small posy vase by
Torquay Pottery, rest by Watcombe.

## Time to thin out superfluous pots

With all collections there eventually comes a time when some pieces are superfluous and need to be thinned out. This can be a painful process especially when the pots bring back memories of happy hunting days at antique or boot fairs and the delight at finding a new treasure (even if it was cracked). Some pots will take pride of place in a collection no matter how battered or chipped simply because they were "Granny's favourite teapot" or the very first piece of Torquay ever purchased. However, other damaged pots, or poorly decorated items can spoil the appearance of a collection and it is time to move them on. One way of "easing the pain" is to remove them from the display and put in the shed for a few months. Some pieces will creep back indoors but others will not be missed and can be sold – remember, your outgrown pots will soon be someone else's treasure.

Whatever you decide to collect it will be special to you as an expression of your personality. Have the courage to collect what you like, not simply to follow current fashions or as an investment – such collections *may* bring financial reward but they will rarely be as spiritually rewarding. Collecting is a hobby which should be fun – enjoy it.

# Devon Cream Teas

**D**EVON was famous for its scenery, cider and cream, and much of the appeal of Torquay cottagewares was that they evoked memories of happy holidays there. A Watcombe advertisement of 1957 stated "Sunshine all the year round. Happy Devon holidays reflected in the ready sales of the original Devon Motto Ware". Many Devon coun-

Fig. 89 Watcombe giant 8 pint teapot decorated with cottages under an amber glaze. These were often used to advertise teashops. The lettering is very elaborate on this example.

Fig. 90 Globular teapot made by the Devon Tors
Pottery to advertise Pear Tree Cafe, Ashburton

try folk converted their front parlour
into a tea room to indulge the visitors
passion for cream teas in picturesque
settings; often the tearoom displayed a
giant teapot in the window to invite
visitors to "Take a cup of tea, its very
refreshing" (fig. 89). Cottages had picturesque names too, such as "Rose Cottage" or "Primrose Cottage" and some,
like Peartree Cottage at Ashburton,
sold their own souvenir wares for customers to take home (fig. 90).

Yet beneath this air of tranquillity
and peace, there was keen competition
between cottages for who produced the
*best* Devon tea – and even debate about
what "tea should consist of". The typical Devon tea was scones with jam and
cream plus a good pot of tea – the ques-
tion was, should you butter the scones
or not? Some locals say yes, butter the
scones, add jam (strawberry or rasp-
berry) then cream on top. Others say no,
put cream on first then jam on top. Don't
ask the Devonians today, either – the
debate continues and can become
heated! Either way, the teas are de-
licious, but don't count the calories.

# Devon and Dorset Potteries that made Cottagewares

**Watcombe Pottery Co.**, St. Marychurch, Torquay.
Established 1869 as the Watcombe Terracotta Company; became Watcombe Pottery Co. in 1884 and in 1901 it was acquired by Hexter Humpherson and Co., who already owned Aller Vale, and combined as the Royal Aller Vale and Watcombe Art Potteries. The two potteries operated independently, although there was some interchange of personnel.
Watcombe made faience style cottages 1906–7 to 1930's; slip decorated cottages from c. 1915 until the pottery closed in 1962.
Also known as Royal Watcombe Pottery.

**Aller Vale Art Potteries**, Kingskerswell, Newton Abbot.
Established as an art pottery in 1881 on a site already used for domestic terracotta.
No evidence of any pigment decorated wares at all. Slip decorated cottages from c. 1915 to c. 1924 when the pottery closed.

Fig. 91 Charlie Wonnacott at the potters wheel, Watcombe Pottery late 1930s. He made mottowares right through to the 1950s.

**Torquay Pottery Company**, Hele Cross, Torquay.
Established 1874 as the Torquay Terracotta Company; c. 1905 it became the Torquay Pottery Co. Ltd., and in 1932 it closed and re-opened as Torquay Pottery (1932) Ltd. Closed c. 1945.
Faience style cottagewares from c. 1908 to c. 1930.
Slip decorated cottagewares from c. 1920–1939.
Moulded Devon cottagewares c. 1914–1939.
Usually known as Royal Torquay Pottery.

**Longpark Pottery Co. Ltd.**, Newton Road, Torquay.
Established c. 1903 on the site of earlier terracotta works; became a limited company in 1905, the directors being G. W. Bond, G. H. Causey, F. H. Blackler, W. J. Skinner, R. H. Skinner and H.E. Bulley. In the Second World War the company was acquired by the Watcombe Pottery and was eventually closed in 1957.
Faience cottagewares c. 1908–1930's.
Slip decorated cottages c. 1918–1957.
A few slip decorated rural scenes with haystacks, cottages, cows and chickens were made c. 1908–1914.
Wares often marked as Royal Longpark Pottery, and Tormohun Ware.

**Hart and Moist, Royal Devon Art Pottery**, Haven Road, St. Thomas, Exeter.
Established 1891 as the Exeter Art Pottery; taken over as Hart and Moist in 1896 and closed in 1933.
Slip decorated cottagewares 1912–1932.

**Crown Dorset Art Potteries**, Green Road, Poole, Dorset.
Company started in 1905 by Charles Collard, who had worked in the Torquay and Exeter potteries.
Pigment decorated (faience) cottages, many in "soft focus" style from c. 1906–7.
Slip decorated cottages from c. 1912–13.
1915 Charles Collard left to start another pottery in Honiton; the Dorset pottery continued to 1925 but the range and quality of wares declined.

**Tor Vale/Lemon and Crute/Daison**, Teignmouth Road, Torquay.
Tor Vale Pottery started in 1913; in 1914 Harry Crute and Tom Lemon acquired the premises as Lemon and Crute; in 1926 Tom Lemon left to go to Weston super Mare and Harry Crute continued to 1931 as the Daison Art Pottery. No known examples of faience style cottages.
Cyril Lemon, son of Tom Lemon, says Lemon and Crute made a few cottagewares in their early days although no identifiable pieces have been seen. Lemon and Crute, and Daison did a few named buildings, including cottages such as the Umbrella Cottage at Lyme Regis; these were on a blue ground.

**Forster and Hunt, the Otter Vale Art Pottery**, High Street, Honiton.
Date of formation of pottery not known, but it went into liquidation in December 1915. Ellis Sydney Forster then went to Torquay and helped found Barton Pottery.
Slip decorated cottages c. 1913–1915.

Fig. 92 Dartmouth c. 1948.

Fig. 93 Devon Tors c. 1925.

**Honiton Pottery**, High Street, Honiton.
Started 1918 by Charles Collard in premises of Forster and Hunt. Early wares in Crown Dorset/Torquay styles, but in the early 1920's these were abandoned in favour of brighter pigments and a matt glaze. Collard retired in 1947 but the Honiton pottery still exists today.
Slip decorated cottages c. 1918–1921.

**Barton Pottery**, Barton Road, St. Marychurch, Torquay.
Started 1921 as H. F. Jackson and Co., Mayville Pottery, the directors being Harry Fletcher Jackson, John Bradford, Alfred George Macey, Ellis Sydney Forster and Alexander Gilbert Hudson. In August 1922 it became Barton Pottery Ltd. which was closed in March 1934 and immediately re-opened as Barton Potteries (1934) Ltd.; this company went into receivership in May 1938. Moonlight scene cottages painted in black pigments on royal blue ground.

**Devon Tors Pottery**, Newton Road, Bovey Tracey.
Established c. 1920 by Robert Fry, William Bond and Frank Bond; closed in the 1970's.
Slip decorated cottage mottowares 1920's and 1930's, and some in post World War II period.
Moulded cottages 1920's and 1930's.

**Devonmoor Art Pottery**, Liverton, Newton Abbot.
Established in 1922 by Herford Hope on site of old Liverton Pottery; after Hope's death during World War II it

became a limited company and eventually closed c. 1977.
Cigarette boxes in form of Anne Hathaway's Cottage from late 1920's, also series of 14 miniature cottages, and some larger models, e.g. First and Last House at Land's End – these were introduced c. 1930 and continued after World War II to c. 1960.

**Bovey Tracey Art Pottery**, Bovey Tracey.
A subsidiary of the Torquay Pottery Company. From c. 1923 to c. 1930 it appears to have operated as part of the Torquay Pottery Co. and sometime in the early 1930's it was made into a separate business under V. A. and M. Kane. Closed c. 1946.
Slip decorated cottages and moulded cottagewares identical to Torquay Pottery Co.

**Plymouth Pottery Co. Ltd.**, Gas House Lane, Coxside, Plymouth.
Established c. 1926 by H. J. Gee, H. J. Gee jnr., A. Yeo and H.E. Turner; seems to have gone out of business c. 1928.
Slip decorated cottagewares.
Usually known as Plymouth Gas Fired pottery.

**Bovey Tracey Pottery Company Ltd.**, Bovey Tracey.
Established in 1840's making white earthenware domestic wares, hand painted or transfer printed; closed 1958.
Some pigment painted cottagewares made in 1930's; these were often known as Dartmoor Ware.

Fig. 94 Decorating shop at the Dartmouth Pottery c. 1948; most of the pots are cottagewares. Reproduced by permission of Dartmouth Pottery.

Fig. 95 Dartmouth Pottery c. 1948;

**Dartmouth Pottery Ltd.**, Warfleet, Dartmouth.
Established 1948 to make slip decorated wares in the Torquay style; still in operation.
Slip decorated cottages 1948–1960's.
In the mid 1950's the company began to make slip cast wares with plain glazes; in the 1960's they gave up handthrown wares altogether.

**Devonshire Potteries Ltd.**, Bovey Tracey.
Established 1948 on site of Bovey Tracey Art Pottery; director was V. A. Kane who was at the earlier pottery too.
Slip decorated cottages 1948–late 1950's.

**Babbacombe Pottery Ltd.**, Babbacombe Road, Torquay.
Established 1952 by E. D. Barrett previously of the Sterling Pottery Ltd., Staffordshire to make slip decorated wares. Peter Priddoe, who had been employed at Dartmouth Pottery, became Chief Designer.
Slip decorated cottagewares 1952–early 1960's.

**St. Marychurch Pottery**, High Street, St. Marychurch, Torquay.
Established 1962 by the Wilson brothers, ex-Watcombe employees, to carry on making traditional Torquay wares.
Slip decorated cottages 1962–1969 when the pottery closed.

Fig. 96 Bovey Tracey, Pottery Road, notice the kilns in the background.

POTTERY ROAD.

WATCOMBE

DEVON
MOTTO
WARE
REG: No.

ENGLAND

C. 1918 — 1928

TORMOHUN
WARE

1903 — 1914

LONGPARK
TORQUAY
ENGLAND

1947- 1957

C. 1935 — 1962

ST. MARYCHURCH
POTTERY

1962 — 1964

ALLER
VALE

C. 1910

BOVEY TRACEY

ART POTTERY

1923 — 1939

Aller Vale

Devon

C. 1902 — 1924

DEVON
TORS
POTTERY

1922- 1939

HELE CROSS
POTTERY
TORQUAY

1905 — 1918

DARTMOUTH
DEVON
ENGLAND

1948- 1960

1928- 1932

ROYAL
TORQUAY
POTTERY
ENGLAND

1924-1939

1918 - 1933

DARTMOOR
WARE

1930's

**H M EXETER**

1900 - 1915

F.H.
Honiton

c. 1915

DARTMOUTH
DEVON

MADE
IN
ENGLAND

1948- 1960

COLLARD
POOLE
DORSET

1905- 1909

1950's

The mottoes that are listed in this book have all been seen on cottagewares. Although they are attributed to a particular pottery, many of them were used by several, or even all, the potteries so collectors should not use the mottoes as a means of identifying unmarked pots.

# Watcombe Mottoes

Nort but taters   (on a pasty)

Who burnt the tablecloth?
(on an ashtray)

He also serves who only stands and waits

Du'ee drink a cup o' Tea

Success comes not by wishing
But by hard work bravely done

Enough's as good as a feast

May the hinges of friendship never go rusty

A creaking gate hangs a long time

Brevity is the soul of wit –
Shakespeare

Ill blows the wind that profits nobody
– Shakespeare

Piping Pebworth, Dancing Marston
Haunted Hillbro', Hungry Grafton
Dodging Exhall, Papist Wixford
Beggarly Broom and Drunken Bidford
                    Shakespeare

When you finish pouring tea
Place the teapot down on me
(on a teapot stand)

Hope well and have well

Little Tommy Tucker
Sings for his supper

Humpty Dumpty
Sat on a wall

Hey diddle diddle

Mary had a little lamb

Hickory Dickory Dock

Simple Simon met a pieman

Tom Tom the Piper's son

Little Jack Horner

Jack and Jill

For a Good Girl

For my dolly

A hair on the head is worth two on the chin   (on a shaving mug)

Here's to beef steak when you're
    hungry
Beer when you're dry
Fivers when you're hard up
Heaven when you die

Hot and strong   (on a mustard pot)

There's a time for all things

Actions speak louder than words

Don't worry it may never happen

Better wait on the cook than the
doctor

Wilful waste makes woeful want

Speak little Speak well

Daun'ee be afraid o' ut now

Say little but think much

There's no time like the present

God hath often a great share in a little
home

To a friend's house, the road is never
long

Do what you can
Being what you are
Shine like a glowworm
If you can't be a star

The cup that cheers

Isn't your life extremely flat
With nothing whatever to grumble at

Some hae meat an canna eat
an some wad eat that want it
But we hae meat an we can eat
Sae let the Lord be thank it

Don't worry and get wrinkles
Smile and have dimples

A saucepan though I be
The fire's not meant for me
But as I'm no use as I am
You'd better fill me up with jam
(on a jam dish shaped like a saucepan)

Love your enemies
Trust but few
And always paddle your own canoe

Zend us a line
Us baint dade    (on an ink well)

O wad some power
The giftie gie us
To see oursels
As ithers see us

Work on Hope on
Self help is noble schooling
You do your best and leave the rest
To Gold Almighty's ruling

Fairest gems lie deepest

If you your lips would keep from slips
Five things observe with care
Of whom you speak, to whom you
speak
And how and when and where.

Many a man sends his wife away for a
    Rest
Because *He* needs it

Don't give your husband too much
    rope
He might skip

Nuts are given us
But we must crack them ourselves

You may get better cheer
But not with better heart

Life is made of time
Don't waste it

A Cornish Litany
From Ghoulies and Ghosties
And Long leggity beasties
And things that go bump in the night
Good Lord deliver us

Niver stray fra' t'home pasture when
    wed

Full many a shaft at random sent
Finds mark the Archer never meant
And many a word at random spoken
Can wound or heal a heart that's
    broken

Life is mostly froth and bubble
Two things stand as stone
Kindness in another's trouble
Courage in your own

If you want zum Biscuits
Ere they be   (on a biscuit barrel)

A fellow feeling makes us wondrous
    kind
But I wonder if the Poet would change
    his mind
If in a crowd one day he were to find
A fellow feeling in his coat behind

The taste of the kitchen is better than
the smell

Take a cup of tea

Better to sit still than rise to fall

I like Zyder
Zyder likes me
I'll drink Zyder
As long as I Kin zee

Good courage breaks ill luck

Do all the good you can
By all the means you can

Take a little butter

The old goose plays not with Foxes

I am an airman        1900
No swallows cant kaitch me   (on a
pint mug made about 1920 – a
personalised motto)

Don't put a good cargo in a poor ship

A car on the road is worth two in the
ditch

I eat my own lamb
My own chickens and ham
I shear my own fleece and wear it
So Jolly boys now
Here's God speed the plough
Long life and success to the farmer

There's a saying old and musty
Yet it is ever true
Tis never trouble trouble
Till trouble troubles you

A hungry man is an angry man

Send us a scrape o' yer pen
(on an inkwell)

If each man in its measure
Would do another's part
To cast a ray of sunshine
Into another's heart

We eat to live not live to eat

When you're in a hurry take your time

Have some sweets

Straight is the line of duty
Curved is the line of beauty
Follow the first and thou shalt see
The second ever following thee

If you're not a beauty
Be happy that you're plain
Be a wheel greaser
If you can't drive a train

Yer's a nice cup a coffee for 'ee

Tis better to wear out than rust out

When you use this shaving pot
Be sure you have the water hot

A flea will bite
Whoi ivver it can
A soa' my lads
Will a Yorkshireman

I cum frum Babbacombe
(on a faience bowl)

# Crown Dorset Mottoes

However lonesome we mid be
The trees would still be company

The friends thou hast and their
   adoption tried
Grapple them to thy heart with hoops
   of steel

Good luck to the Hoof an the Harn
Good luck to the Flock an the Fleece
Good luck to the growers of Carn
Wi blessens of Plenty an Peace

Save while you have and give while
you live

Contentment is a constant feast
(Barnes)

# Longpark Mottoes

Make hay while the sun shines

Drink like a fish
Water only

Fresh from the dairy

Be aisy wid the cream

Tis deeds alone must win the prize

Hear all   See all   Say nothing

Dawntee try tu rin
Bevore yu kin walk

Dawntee vall bevore yu'm pushed

The man that can't make a mistake
Can't make anything

I'll take care of the pins
(on a hair pin tray)

When you want to kill time
Work it to death

A pound of pluck is worth a ton of luck

A match for any man
(on a match holder)

# Dartmouth Mottoes

No road is long with good company

Us be always plaised to zee 'ee

To thine own self be true

Go aisy wi' it now

Time and Tide wait for no man

Many friends few helpers

Many hands make light work

Naught venture, naught have

A rolling stone gathers no moss

Ill blows the wind that profits nobody

None are so good as they should be

Never say die
Up man and try

Be like the sundial
Count only the sunny hours

Georgie Porgie Pudden and Pie kissed
the Girls   (on a child's dish)

Drink up me arty an 'ave some more

Within this jug there is good liquor
Fit for parson or for Vicar
How to dring and not to spill
Will try the utmost of your Skill
(transfer printed on a puzzle jug)

# Babbacombe Mottoes

Little ships must keep to shore
Larger vessels venture more

Waste not   Want not

When your head feels queer
And your breath smells strong
And you laugh like hell at any old
song
Your drunk old man, you're drunk

More haste less speed

# Hart and Moist Mottoes

Look before you leap

Home the spot on earth supremely
blest

# Honiton Mottoes

Lest we forget

Is the tea tae yer likin?

Always merry and bright

Hope shall brighten days to come
And memory gild the past

# Plymouth Mottoes

Good counsel has no price

East or West, Home's best

A friend in need is a friend indeed

# Torquay Pottery Mottoes

Say it with flowers   (on a vase)

Barking dogs seldom bite

# Aller Vale Mottoes

Never trouble trouble
Till trouble troubles you

Actions speak louder than words

# Welsh Mottoes

Cymru am byth (Wales for ever)

Ychydig o Laeth (a little milk)

Llaeth y fuwch (The cows milk)

Dim melus fel siwgr (Nothing sweetens like sugar)

Ar ol Gorphen Tywallt Rhowch
Y Tebod Yn Ei Le (After pouring the tea put the teapot in its place)

Anrheg o Gymru (A present from Wales)

Bwthyn Cymreig (Welsh cottage)

Bore da (Good morning)

O geiniog i geiniog ar arian yn bunt (Look after the pennies and the pounds will look after themselves)

Right.  Fig. 97 is taken from a Watcombe catalogue c. 1928 but unfortunately the prices were missing. The following prices are from a later catalogue, c. 1935, which showed a similar range of items.

Butter tub, no. 1513, made in 3 sizes from 10/- to 15/- dozen
Tall candlestick, no. 1467, made in 4 sizes from 4″ tall @ 10/- to 10″ tall @ 36/- dozen
Teapot, no. 1476, made in 4 sizes from 11/- to 30/- dozen
Short candleholder, no. 146, 8/- per dozen
Jam dish, no. 80, made in 2 sizes @ 9/- and 12/- dozen
Egg cup with saucer not available in 1935; egg cups shown were of the pedestal or tub variety.
(Note: £1 = 20/-)

# Wholesale Prices of Watcombe Mottowares November 1958

Barrel jug, made in 3 sizes @ 28/-, 41/9, 64/- per dozen
Cruet on stand 81/6 doz.
Triple tray 81/6 doz.
Double jam 68/6 doz.
Cream bowl 48/6 doz.
Tyg, 2″ @ 18/6 doz. 3″ @ 23/- doz.
Named ware 5% extra
(Note: £1 = 20/-)

Right.  Fig. 98 From a Watcombe catalogue c. 1958. Note how the quality of decoration has declined especially on the trefoil dish (compare with fig. 48).

1513A     1467     1476

146     88     80

COTTAGE.  MOTTO.

ORIGINAL DEVON MOTTO WARE

88

# Watcombe Country Life View Ware Wholesale prices c. 1910

Teapot, shape no. 137 (as shown in fig. 4), made in 4 sizes from 18/- to 66/- per dozen
Vase, shape no. 164 (as shown on inside front cover), made in 6 sizes:
4½" @ 12/-   6" 18/-   8" @ 30/-   10" @ 66/-   12" @ 90/-   14" @ 120/-
all prices per dozen items

# Winter Cottage Ware 1958 prices

Plates, made in 6 sizes from 4" @ 14/6 dozen, to 9" @ 54/3 dozen
Teapot, made in 4 sizes from 57/- dozen to 136/- dozen
Cups and saucers, made in 3 sizes from 32/- to 44/6 dozen
(Note: £1 = 20/-)

# First and Last House

Land's End is the most western point of the English mainland; it is a rugged granite peninsula with steep cliffs which drop down into turbulent seas. The area is popular with tourists because of its stories of shipwrecks, smugglers and Cornish piskies! The lonely cottage known as the "First and Last House in England" caters for the holidaymakers, selling refreshments, as well as an abundance of souvenirs and postcards.

# Clovelly

Clovelly is a delightful village on the north Devon coast, nine miles west of Bideford. It is sometimes described as a "waterfall" because of the way the main cobbled street drops down 400 feet in steps towards the sea – transport is by foot, sledge or donkey. Flower decked cottages cling to the sides of the road, vying with each other to be the most picturesque and photogenic. Many cottages were popular views for souvenir ware, such as Crazy Kate's Cottage and Rose Cottage.

# Anne Hathaway's Cottage

Anne Hathaway's Cottage is in the village of Shottery, a mile from Stratford on Avon. It dates from the fifteenth century and is a timber framed building with brick, stone and wattle walls under a thatched roof. The "cottage" is really a large 12 roomed house set in a typical English country garden which is a blaze of colour in the summer. Anne Hathaway lived in the house until her marriage to William Shakespeare around 1582.

# Burns' Cottage

Robert Burns was born in a small cottage at Alloway, two miles south of Ayr, on 25th January 1759. The cottage was built by his father, who was an agricultural worker, and the young "Robbie" spent the first seven years of his life there. It is now a museum and popular tourist attraction.

Fig. 99 Fred Dart who worked at Aller Vale and Watcombe Potteries.

Fig. 100 Devon Tors

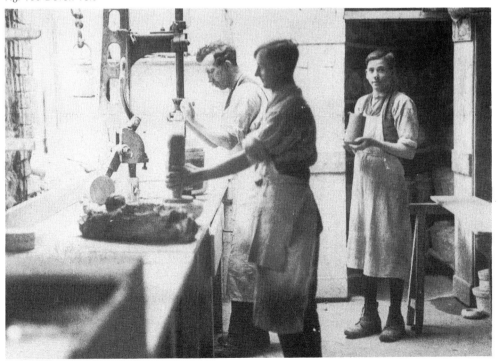

Fig. 101 Watcombe jardiniere and stand 39" (100 cms) tall c. 1910.